30 Quotes to Color
DIY BOOK

Quote & Cupcake Coloring Bookmarks

free download coloring pages

At : bit.ly/get_sample_free

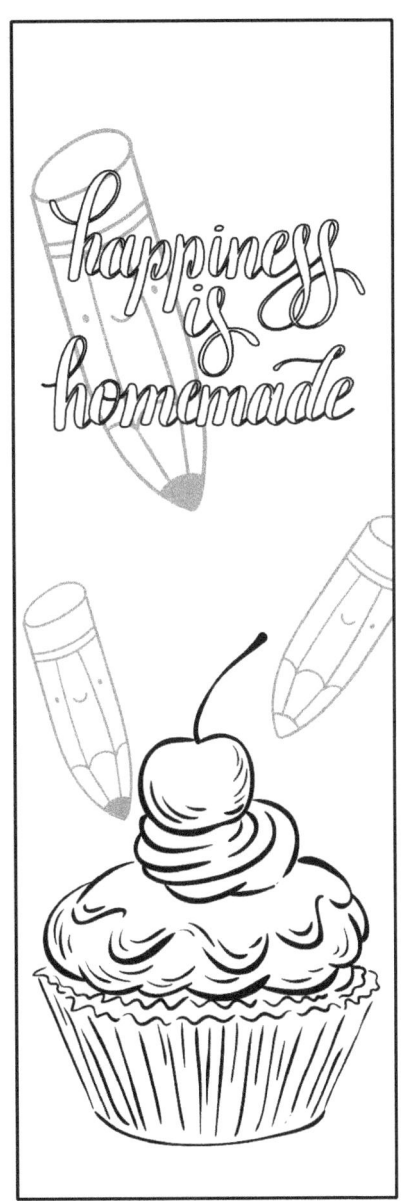

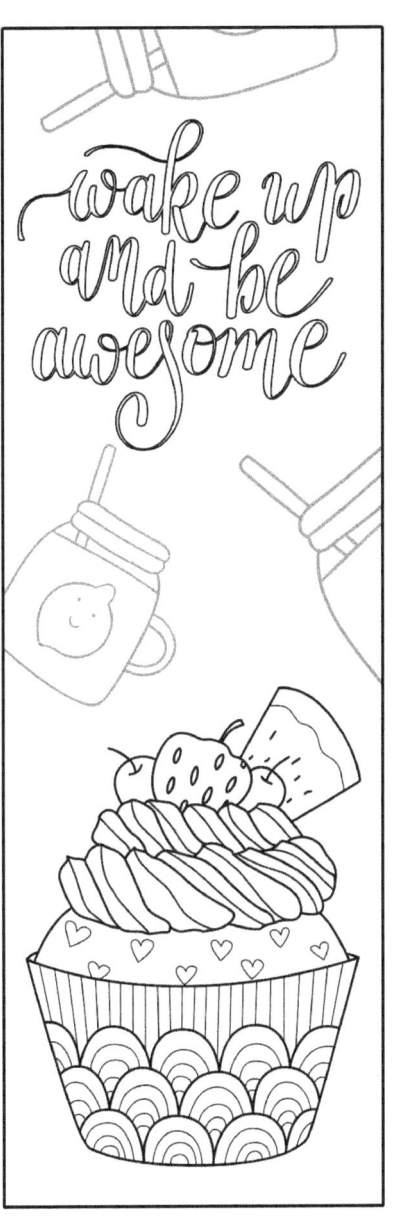

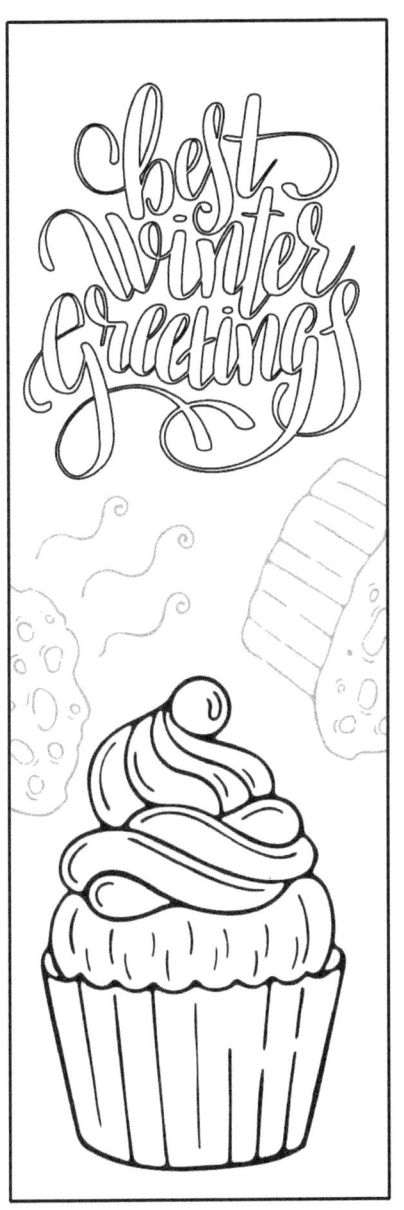

CPSIA information can be obtained
at www.ICGtesting.com
Printed in the USA
LVHW080218071118
596278LV00014B/555/P